THE HAUNTED!

HAUNTED
GRAVEYARDS
AND TEMPLES

A Crabtree Branches Book

THOMAS KINGSLEY TROUPE

CRABTREE
Publishing Company
www.crabtreebooks.com

School-to-Home Support for Caregivers and Teachers

This high-interest book is designed to motivate striving students with engaging topics while building fluency, vocabulary, and an interest in reading. Here are a few questions and activities to help the reader build upon his or her comprehension skills.

Before Reading:
- *What do I think this book is about?*
- *What do I know about this topic?*
- *What do I want to learn about this topic?*
- *Why am I reading this book?*

During Reading:
- *I wonder why...*
- *I'm curious to know...*
- *How is this like something I already know?*
- *What have I learned so far?*

After Reading:
- *What was the author trying to teach me?*
- *What are some details?*
- *How did the photographs and captions help me understand more?*
- *Read the book again and look for the vocabulary words.*
- *What questions do I still have?*

Extension Activities:
- *What was your favorite part of the book? Write a paragraph on it.*
- *Draw a picture of your favorite thing you learned from the book.*

TABLE OF CONTENTS

HOLY, BUT HAUNTED!

Crooked headstones glow in the moonlight. Wind whistles through the tall grass like a whisper. The abandoned temple's jagged shadow looms above. It feels like someone is watching you. You shouldn't be here. As you turn, an icy chill races up your back. A faded figure stands near the graveyard gate. There is no escape!

There are haunted locations all over the world. Some believe spirits cling to the real world for **eternity**. Graveyards and temples celebrate the dead, making them the likeliest haunted hot spots.

Grab your flashlight and take a deep breath. You're about to discover why these graveyards and places of worship are among...

THE HAUNTED.

FRIGHTENING FACT

There are over 144,000 graveyards and cemeteries in the United States.

HOLLYWOOD FOREVER CEMETERY

Just like regular people, famous people die too. The Hollywood Forever Cemetery in California is the final resting place for many celebrities.

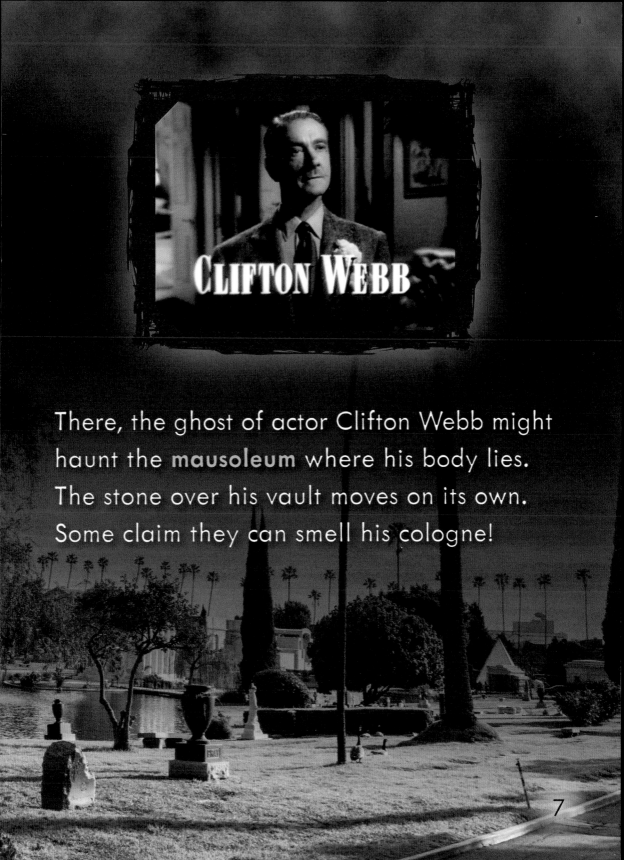

CLIFTON WEBB

There, the ghost of actor Clifton Webb might haunt the **mausoleum** where his body lies. The stone over his vault moves on its own. Some claim they can smell his cologne!

PARIS CATACOMBS

In 18th century Paris, France, there were more corpses than places to bury them. Gravediggers used to bury bodies on top of other bodies. With smelly, decaying corpses everywhere, the city had to do something.

They opened the old limestone mines beneath the city and put the bodies in them. The tunnels became an underground cemetery, or catacomb.

FRIGHTENING FACT

It took 12 years to move all of the bodies from the overstuffed graveyards to the Paris Catacombs.

The catacombs are open for tours, but some believe the tunnels are haunted. They've seen light orbs, heard voices, and spotted strange shadows.

During the French Revolution (1789-1799) Philibert Aspairt stumbled into the tunnels. He got lost and his body was found 11 years later. His ghost often haunts the spot where he died.

A LA MÉMOIRE
DE PHILIBERT ASPAIRT
PERDU DANS CETTE
CARRIÈRE LE III NOV^BRE
MDCCXCIII RETROUVÉ
ONZE ANS APRÈS ET
INHUMÉ EN LA MÊME PLACE
LE XXX AVRIL MDCCCIV

The bones of over 6 million Parisians are stored in the Paris Catacombs.

ST. LOUIS CEMETERY NO. 1

Things are done differently in New Orleans, Louisiana. In their St. Louis Cemetery No. 1, the dead are buried in above-ground vaults.

It's considered the most haunted graveyard in the United States. The ghost of **Voodoo** Queen Marie Laveau often walks among the tombs. Some visitors report they've been scratched, pinched, and pushed to the ground.

Queen Marie Laveau

FRIGHTENING FACT

There are 700 tombs and more than 100,000 bodies in St. Louis Cemetery No. 1.

ROOKWOOD CEMETERY, AUSTRALIA

In Australia, the Land Down Under, there is a **necropolis** known as Rookwood Cemetery. This huge place is the final resting place of over one million people.

Two **spiritualists** known as the Davenport Brothers are buried there. Many believe ghosts are drawn to the cemetery because of the Davenports.

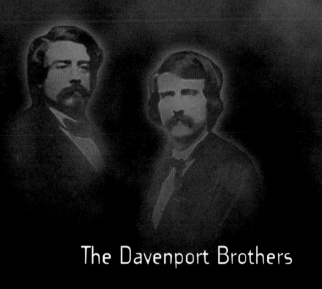
The Davenport Brothers

MASONIC TEMPLE, DETROIT

Ghosts don't always haunt the places where their bodies are buried. In Detroit, Michigan, a Masonic Temple is believed to be haunted.

Architect George D. Mason designed
the enormous temple and died there
many years later. Visitors have spotted
his ghost climbing the steps. Others
have seen doors slam shut on their own.

FRIGHTENING FACT

The Masonic Temple contains secret rooms
and passageways. It even has an unfinished
swimming pool on the 6th floor.

ST. ANDREWS ON THE RED, CANADA

Winnipeg, Manitoba, in Canada is home to St. Andrews on the Red, an old church and graveyard. Many who died from diseases in the past were buried there.

Some claim St. Andrews is haunted by a woman in white and a man in black. Still others witnessed a phantom car with glowing red eyes.

SAN FERNANDO CATHEDRAL,
SAN ANTONIO, TEXAS

The San Fernando Cathedral in San Antonio, Texas, is the state's oldest church. During its construction, Spanish settlers battled the area's Apache people.

In 1749, a peace offering was made. The Apaches dug a large hole in front of the cathedral. They buried arrows, **hatchets**, and a white horse that was still alive.

FRIGHTENING FACT

The expression "bury the hatchet" came from the burial of native weapons. It was considered a gesture of peace.

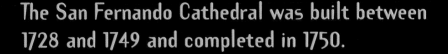

The San Fernando Cathedral was built between 1728 and 1749 and completed in 1750.

Now considered a historic place, the cathedral is a haunted haven. Strange glowing lights and mysterious shadows have been spotted.

A ghostly white horse sometimes gallops through the site. Many believe it is the spirit of the horse that was buried alive in front of the cathedral.

CATHEDRAL OF THE ASSUMPTION OF OUR LADY, GUADALAJARA, MEXICO

Are the oldest places of worship the most haunted? Is seems true for the Cathedral of the Assumption of our Lady. Located in Guadalajara, Mexico, it was built in sections from 1535 to 1813.

Below the cathedral's greater **altar** is the Crypt of the Archbishops. There, they keep the bones and mummified bodies of **bishops** and **cardinals**.

FRIGHTENING FACT

Parishioners would place their hands on the coffins of dead bishops and ask for favors. If they put their ear to the coffin and heard an answer, their wish would be granted.

Some of the bodies in the cathedral's crypt don't seem ready to leave the land of the living. One of the bodies is of a child killed for her religious beliefs in the 1700s. People claim to have seen the girl's eyes blink and her hair move.

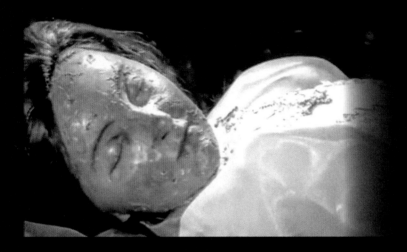

FRIGHTENING FACT

We call mummified bodies, mummies. Mummies are dead bodies that have been preserved naturally, or by ancient peoples skilled in mummification.

CONCLUSION

It's hard to say if ghosts truly do haunt graveyards and temples. What one person sees, another might explain away.

It's up to you to decide for yourself. If you hear or see something creepy, write it down or capture it with a camera. The evidence you discover might bring us closer to understanding...THE HAUNTED.

GLOSSARY

altar (AWL-tur): A platform or table used as a center for worship

architect (AR-ki-tekt): A person who designs buildings

bishops (BISH-uhps): Religious leaders for Christian churches

cardinals (KAR-duh-nuhlz): High officials of the Roman Catholic Church

eternity (i-TUR-nuh-tee): A period of time that seems endless

hatchets (HACH-its): Small axes with short handles

mausoleum (maw-suh-LEE-uhm): A stone building where dead bodies are kept in vaults

necropolis (nuh-KRAH-pul-uhs): A large cemetery with tomb monuments. Also a Greek word that means "city of the dead".

spiritualists (SPIHR-uh-chool-ists): People who believe the spirits of the dead can communicate with living people

Voodoo (VOO-doo): A religion practiced in the Caribbean and southern United States

INDEX

WEBSITES TO VISIT

https://kids.kiddle.co/Ghost

www.hauntedrooms.co.uk/ghost-
stories-kids-scary-childrens

www.ghostsandgravestones.com/
how-to-ghost-hunt

ABOUT THE AUTHOR

Thomas Kingsley Troupe

Thomas Kingsley Troupe is the author of a whole pile of books for kids. He's written about ghosts, Bigfoot, werewolves, and even a book about dirt. When he's not writing or reading, he investigates the paranormal as part of the Twin Cities Paranormal Society. He lives in Woodbury, Minnesota with his 2 sons.

CRABTREE
Publishing Company

Produced by: Blue Door Education for Crabtree Publishing
Written by: Thomas Kingsley Troupe
Designed by: Jennifer Dydyk
Edited by: Kelli Hicks
Proofreader: Crystal Sikkens

The images/photos depicting "ghosts" in this book are artists' interpretations. The publisher does not claim these are actual images/photos taken of the ghosts mentioned in this book.

Cover photos: skull on cover and throughout book ©Fer Gregory, graveyard © Fer Gregory, girl © kittirat roekburi, pg.s 4-5 cemetery © Fahroni, old temple © SHELIAKIN MAKSIM, pg. 5 creepy picture border © Dmitry Natashin, pg.s 6-7 cemetery © Alizada Studios, pg. 8 © Netfalls Remy Musser, pg. 9 background photo © Ilias Kouroudis, photo border art here and throughout book © Dmitry Natashin, top photo © Mikhail Gnatkovskiy, photo showing carvings © Spirit Stock, pg. 10 background photo © Spirit Stock, top photo © Stas Guk, pg. 11 ghost © Tereshchenko Dmitry, pg. 12 background photo © Pg. Light Studios, inset photo © Pg. Light Studios, pg. 13 angel © Scott A . Burns, pg. 14 © Ms S. Ann, pg. 15 bottom photo © ArliftAtoz2205, pg. 16 © Fsendek, pg. 17 both photos © Belikova Oksana, pg. 19 © Raggedstone, pg. 20 © fllphoto, pg. 21 hatchet © Barandash Karandashich, pg. 22 horse © mariait, pg. 23 © CrackerClips Stock Media, pg. 24 © Nara_money, pg. 26 (bottom) Editorial credit: Ecuadorpostales / Shutterstock.com, pg. 27 © Adwo, pg. 28 © Carlos Amarillo, pg. 29 © Raggedstone. All images from Shutterstock.com except pg. 7 Clifton Webb, public domain image, pg. 11 Philibert Aspairt tomb © Rémi Villalongue (Wikimedia https://creativecommons.org/licenses/by-sa/3.0/deed.en), pg. 13 Marie Laveau public domain image by Smerdis of Tlön, pg. 15 Davenport Brothers courtesy of the Library of Congress, pg. 18 © Dig deeper Wikipedia https://creativecommons.org/licenses/by-sa/4.0/deed.en, pg. 25 (top) © Kobby Dagan | Dreamstime.com, pg. 26 (top) © Enciclopedia1993 https://creativecommons.org/licenses/by-sa/4.0/deed.en

Library and Archives Canada Cataloguing in Publication
Title: Haunted graveyards and temples / Thomas Kingsley Troupe.
Names: Troupe, Thomas Kingsley, author.
Description: Series statement: The haunted! | "A Crabtree branches book". | Includes index.
Identifiers: Canadiana (print) 2021022018X |
    Canadiana (ebook) 20210220198 |
    ISBN 9781427155542 (hardcover) |
    ISBN 9781427155603 (softcover) |
    ISBN 9781427155665 (HTML) |
    ISBN 9781427155726 (EPUB) |
    ISBN 9781427155788 (read-along ebook)
Subjects: LCSH: Haunted cemeteries—Juvenile literature. |
    LCSH: Haunted places—Juvenile literature.
    | LCSH: Temples—Juvenile literature. | LCSH: Ghosts—Juvenile literature.
Classification: LCC BF1474.3 .T76 2022 | DDC j133.1/22—dc23

Library of Congress Cataloging-in-Publication Data
Names: Troupe, Thomas Kingsley, author.
Title: Haunted graveyards and temples / Thomas Kingsley Troupe.
Description: New York, NY : Crabtree Publishing Company, [2022] |
    Series: The haunted! - a Crabtree Branches book | Includes index.
Identifiers: LCCN 2021022532 (print) |
    LCCN 2021022533 (ebook) |
    ISBN 9781427155542 (hardcover) |
    ISBN 9781427155603 (paperback) |
    ISBN 9781427155665 (ebook) |
    ISBN 9781427155726 (epub) |
    ISBN 9781427155788
Subjects: LCSH: Haunted cemeteries--Juvenile literature. | Haunted temples--Juvenile literature. | Ghosts--Juvenile literature.
Classification: LCC BF1474.3 .T76 2022 (print) | LCC BF1474.3 (ebook) | DDC 133.1/22--dc23
LC record available at https://lccn.loc.gov/2021022532
LC ebook record available at https://lccn.loc.gov/2021022533

Crabtree Publishing Company
www.crabtreebooks.com   1-800-387-7650

Copyright © 2022 **CRABTREE PUBLISHING COMPANY**

Published in the United States
Crabtree Publishing
347 Fifth Avenue, Suite 1402-145
New York, NY, 10016

Published in Canada
Crabtree Publishing
616 Welland Ave.
St. Catharines, ON, L2M 5V

Printed in the U.S.A./072021/CG20210514